Tall Dot

by Rick Kristoff
illustrated by Hector Borlasca

Practice Decodable 18

McGraw Hill Education
Bothell, WA • Chicago, IL • Columbus, OH • New York, NY

MHEonline.com

Send all inquiries to:
McGraw-Hill Education
8787 Orion Place
Columbus, OH 43240

ISBN: 978-0-02-130272-7
MHID: 0-02-130272-3

Printed in China.

8 9 10 11 12 DSS 27 26 25 24 23

Dot has a call.

It is Scott, a sad cab man.

Dot is not small. Dot is tall.

Can tall Dot stand and see?

"I see halt and stop!"

Scott is calm and sad.